KINGDOM ANIMALIA

WINNER, 2011 ISABELLA GARDNER POETRY AWARD

KINGDOM ANIMALIA

POEMS BY
ARACELIS GIRMAY

AMERICAN POETS CONTINUUM SERIES, No. 131

BOA EDITIONS, LTD. ❈ ROCHESTER, NY ❈ 2011

First Edition

For information about permission to reuse any material from this book please contact The Permissions Company at www.permissionscompany.com or e-mail permdude@ eclipse.net.

Publications by BOA Editions, Ltd.—a not-for-profit corporation under section 501 (c) (3) of the United States Internal Revenue Code—are made possible with funds from a variety of sources, including public funds from the New York State Council on the Arts, a state agency; the Literature Program of the National Endowment for the Arts; the County of Monroe, NY; the Lannan Foundation for support of the Lannan Translations Selection Series; the Mary S. Mulligan Charitable Trust; the Rochester Area Community Foundation; the Arts & Cultural Council for Greater Rochester; the Steeple-Jack Fund; the Ames-Amzalak Memorial Trust in memory of Henry Ames, Semon Amzalak and Dan Amzalak; and contributions from many individuals nationwide.

See Colophon on page 120 for special individual acknowledgments.

Cover Design: Sandy Knight
Cover Art: Carla Repice
Interior Design and Composition: Richard Foerster
Manufacturing: Bookmobile
BOA Logo: Mirko

Library of Congress Cataloging-in-Publication Data

Girmay, Aracelis.
Kingdom animalia : poems / by Aracelis Girmay. — 1st ed.
    p. cm. — (American poets continuum series ; no. 131)
ISBN 978-1-934414-62-0 (trade pbk.)
I. Title.
PS3607.I47K56 2011
811'.6—dc22
                        2011001428

NATIONAL
ENDOWMENT
FOR THE ARTS
A great nation
deserves great art.

BOA Editions, Ltd.
250 North Goodman Street, Suite 306
Rochester, NY 14607
www.boaeditions.org
A. Poulin, Jr., Founder (1938–1996)

State of the Arts

NYSCA

for Ade Zuphan

Thus, from the war of nature, from famine and death, the most exalted object which we are capable of conceiving, namely, the production of the higher animals, directly follows. There is grandeur in this view of life, with its several powers, having been originally breathed into a few forms or into one; and that, whilst this planet has gone cycling on according to the fixed law of gravity, from so simple a beginning endless forms most beautiful and most wonderful have been, and are being, evolved.

—Charles Darwin, *The Origin of Species*

Contents

iv. a book of erased cities

v. a fable

vi. the book of one small thing

The framework of bones being the same in the hand of a man, wing of a bat, fin of the porpoise, and leg of the horse,—the same number of vertebrae forming the neck of the giraffe and of the elephant,—and innumerable other such facts, at once explain themselves on the theory of descent...

—Charles Darwin, *Origin of Species*

i. a book of dirt

Kingdom Animalia

When I get the call about my brother,
I'm on a stopped train leaving town
& the news packs into me—freight—
though it's him on the other end
now, saying *finefine*—

Forfeit my eyes, I want to turn away
from the hair on the floor of his house
& how it got there Monday,
but my one heart falls
like a sad, fat persimmon
dropped by the hand of the Turczyn's old tree.

I want to sleep. I do not want to sleep. See,

one day, not today, not now, we will be gone
from this earth where we know the gladiolas.
My brother, this noise,
some love [you] I loved
with all my brain, & breath,
will be gone; I've been told, today, to consider this
as I ride the long tracks out & dream so good

I see a plant in the window of the house
my brother shares with his love, their shoes. & there
he is, asleep in bed
with this same woman whose long skin
covers all of her bones, in a city called Oakland,
& their dreams hang above them
a little like a chandelier, & their teeth
flash in the night, oh, body.

Oh, body, be held now by whom you love.
Whole years will be spent, underneath these impossible stars,
when dirt's the only animal who will sleep with you
& touch you with
its mouth.

Elegy

What to do with this knowledge
that our living is not guaranteed?

Perhaps one day you touch the young branch
of something beautiful. & it grows & grows
despite your birthdays & the death certificate,
& it one day shades the heads of something beautiful
or makes itself useful to the nest. Walk out
of your house, then, believing in this.
Nothing else matters.

All above us is the touching
of strangers & parrots,
some of them human,
some of them not human.

Listen to me. I am telling you
a true thing. This is the only kingdom.
The kingdom of touching;
the touches of the disappearing, things.

Abuelo, Mi Muerto

Abuelo, I've walked three nights
in the last city you breathed in,
trying to read every thing:

the birds, the buildings, the rain. & still
no luck, which means nothing
more than I am dense & far from you

though this is your town, your
Sunday-walk haberdashery,
your way back home from the train, & trees

you passed a thousand times
like a child below the gray gaze of its mothers.
How could I be lost here

in your jackal-mouthed, murderous
streets who swallowed your children, Abuelo,
while the church bells marked the parish & hour?

The uncles & aunts strewn
about like funeral carnations—
Sometimes it is so hard to hear you

in the outside language of crows
though my window's an open eye.
Hard to understand

what the hawk is spelling
as it moves just so in the sky:

x

My head is thick, but I know
you are telling me something
when I hear the rooster crow,

or the hawk there circling.
Mostly it's the birds who send me looking
for the lost room of your face. The last memory I have of you

was in El Toro. My mother clipped your toenails
off an old & naked foot, while the other one
slept in a basin on the floor—sluggish

catfish, sleeping fish
like a fisherman's catch. In the bucket,
alive but nearly dying. Do you remember?

Do you remember? This
is my only proof. Memory
tells me I am yours. I am yours,

Abuelo. If the pigeons can wear
the same face in every city,
the same red feet, singing

the same songs & so on & so on,
can't you come back, Abuelo?
Tell me which are the graves

I should visit & clean. Which river
I should bring my flowers to.
Which of the miracles

fills your marigold chest?
Which is the joke you loved the most?
What is the name of the desert

I should thank? Come back
in a body I can see from the window
of this crowded city train.

Board the train. Sit
beside me for a while & tell me things.
Do not let me mistake you

for a shadow or a gull.
& if I start to pass you on the street,
Abuelo, shout my name, shout

it, please. Tug my shirt or hair.
Make me turn. Just a moment.
Send me home with a message

my mother will believe. Wear a body
I can see with my slowest eye. Speak a language
whose words I cannot help but wear

like a family feather
in my black
& grandfather hair.

Dear Minnie, Dear Ms.

for Minnie Riperton & Ms. Lucille

This earth
        of the dagger-toothed & hawks,
whose names we know,
taking bones for diamonds,
        full of hair & snakes,
earth eating you, slowly,
        below the sound
        of gold horns.

This earth
        with a jaw in its hand.
Brown-chariot, take-you-home
earth, chew you up
        with the quiet work
of animals & trees, underworld
        churning you through
        the dark engines
        of its appetite. This

earth we opened up
        & buried you in, our
treasure, we miss
you, we miss you
        with all life. This night
we think we will never close
        again. We are pinned open
        like a scientist's moths
        to leave you there dressed
        in a box & earth around you.
This box earth, coffin
        earth. Teeth earth eat
your chest through, laced

by the wrangle of beetles & worms
       & ants who carry your bright pieces
like market cloth over their heads
      to feed you to the queen
      in the deeper corridors
      of mysteries & dirt.

Trust the queen is you.

Trust the mud is you,
& the soft, silver afro of the dandelion.

Trust the grass-whistle might be
your speech, high as the whistle
of the whale. Trust

we'll know your shape, whatever species
in you answers when we put our faces
to the dirt & call you by
your old & human name.

Small Letter

do not go, this day, the red
of bridges, my little, stay

beside me over
the ruins of san francisco.

go, but do not go
from me, my one,

my love, my very kin
who I laughed with in our sleep

every night, my dream
beside your dream, for a year.

wrecking ball despedida, wreck
the great rooms in my chest & take

my last song, but do not leave me
on this earth, my one

without my one. how would
the hand ever live, if it knew

it would never braid your hair
again, or hold your face?

it would get up & walk
away forever then.

one by one my breaths
would go out looking: a procession

of homeless dogs,

                     or clouds

Zewdit

Because she has a name
in the book of my family, the book

of my father's brain & chest,
because everyone who looks

at the old photograph of the birdish
& beautiful child always says

the same thing: Zewdit.
I believe I have an aunt named Zewdit

whose face I've never seen
without the translation of the camera's

machine, because she is not here,
not any of the people who walk

through the house. Small, like the skeleton
of the sparrow, my father's voice

saying she was gone. Because
I have never met her in our family's houses,

because I never met her on a train or at the hotel
in Frankfurt, on a layover, she was not one of the women there

who looked up from folding the hot blankets
& mopping the floor to kiss my cheeks & kiss

my cheeks when I said Yes! Adis Ogdo.
Because she was not one of them who took me

for tea & accompanied me to the airport the next day
when I said the name of my grandfather's town

though we were thousands of miles away, because
there are no new letters marked with international stamps now,

I believe that she was here once, & has gone—Everything
is the absence of her: if she stands, this morning, with the deer
            outside

the window of this house I borrow, if she stands with the deer,
right now, this cold & April morning, all I see are the deer.

If she laughs with the laughter of crows & other birds
in the morning, all I hear are the crows & other birds.

This world, uninterrupted by her body & her skin, as if,
like in the story of cats, she has brought the great bird of the day
            to my door,

the day, large & great, in her invisible mouth. As if
this world without her face is the only sentence, She has gone.

Starlight Multiplication

for Ade Haragu

It is good to praise god in the body
of the grandmother who is dead. Holy love
of bread & lovers who held your hand
as they kissed the soft meat between your legs, yes
Grandmother, I am singing this song to you,
though the lyrics make you cover your face, I want
you to be kissed again, even if only in songs. Like that.
My head is so full of ideas, I say your name
as I am building the houses
of the city in this poem. I am walking
through the night's alleys,
alleys of stars & crickets saying
your name into the wall where the neighbors moan
in a dark room on the other side of my home.
Grandmother, animals running
through the gates of their lovers, then fields
is old news. It does not pull you from the ground
or wake you from a sleep beneath
old cemetery stones & cactus.
On my life, on mud & starlight,
I want to dress my voice in horses
& send them back 60 years, Haragu,
to stand silver nights outside your marriage window
singing Bless you, Grandmother, in Gondar.
You thought you were dreaming. The red horses you saw
when your husband touched your ankle with his mouth.
What is the sound of two lines crossing? *Haragu*—
What is the word the salt says? *Haragu, Haragu*—
your body & your name here, at first,
then vanishing, like the stars.

Night

for Aboy Keleta

Night, loose
of its blue skin,

scattered with goats,
black & white, across

its dark, flat fields
beside the kitchens singing

with fires not enormous
as the kerosene stoves

skirt the kettles in flames.
There will be this night,

this night sung to by the ox
who, in my sleep, is extraordinary

sound. On the edge of this town
my Aboy sleeps in a dirt room

beneath the dirt. The candles dim,
& the light. I am not far,

not far from that cemetery starred
with his teeth. Compass-blood, push

me out of bed to pass small houses
of my cousins who breathe

as their children dream together on this,
our land, spelled with the blood of mothers & uncles.

Aboy, tonight I cannot tell you from the dirt or the stone
in my shoe that rolls beneath me like a trick. If I stand

in the middle of this red & crumbling road as the wind
blows against me in the open air, my prayer

is for some small piece of my body to fall & fall away.
Again, my dark will be untellable from yours.

On Living

What to do with this knowledge
that our living is not guaranteed?

What could she do? What does one do
when the mother's mouth is gone;
when the mother closes her eye, the door,
but shuts Girl, this time, out—

Girl wanted words,
but there was only sadness
for the big & dreadful death.

What could she do
but swallow loss?

The black & tumbleweed of those nights
became her home beside her sister.
They mother each other, still, like wolves, like any animal
will do, does, once she's found she's been pushed or fallen
out of the grave, to live.

They live. There is nothing left
to do   but live.

ii. a book of beautiful monsters

Swan, As the Light Was Changing

Fall, when everything was turning
dark. & the fog moved in
like a wolf, circling the park,

& the holiday children parading
in the bodies of witches & bears.
All skins gleamed orange

as the sun made tricks out of us,
brilliant as new coins or foxes
until the sun left, all the way,

& the only light, then, was
the white of the swan,
animal in the park pond. So long—

I held it in my eye the way a person
sometimes carries a flash,
again & again; like light, that swan shape burned

into the screen of my eyes. & when I stood
to leave it, the white peony of its body,
for life, had marked my visions. Now everything

I see, even today, even this "trace": a swan.

For Patrick Rosal Who Wore a Dress & Said,

A dude rocks a slick green dress once, for kicks,
& the whole gender paradigm has to shift? Come on.
Haven't you seen the women glide down streets
with frocks so wide you envied them their summer
shimmy, the loose-loose dazzle of their dresses
above knees? Not *just* the knees. But the *dresses*
above the knees. Haven't you wanted to stand at the mirror
as the sister you never had, so bad, you could almost feel
the bird of her voice start to rise inside your own throat? Nightingale.
Listen. Once, in June, the dress was green,
& I flew into it from the diving board of my sex
& I didn't care that the trees were watching. & I didn't care
who saw. In fact, I ran out the door, into the magenta hall
of the Campus Inn hotel where I was visiting, & a poet,
& I laughed & laughed & laughed. I didn't care
that the rooms were full. I didn't care
that people might hear. In fact, I wanted them
to catch me in the lit Technicolor of my glee & mistake me for
a flashlight. Or a discotheque. For a bald & handsome lola
parading my two strong legs through the hall, out
onto the street, singing to strangers
something lovely about the breeze, have
mercy. I wore a dress & it made me nice, yes. Once,
I was a man who stood inside of a dress
& loved it with my whole brain. My body did not change
from its line, before or after. My name did not change, but
I moved into that green, & it was easy—to swing
the regions of my body with new grace
as the street sang up to me from below, *Go on,*
& my hairs stood up like switchgrass
atop the gold fields of my skin, bless
this holy, holy chance to move
above the ground
like this.

March, March

Brown March whose branches itch with coming spring
& the yellow hands of dogwood in the yard.

Obscene, the beauty of skin again, obscene this Eden season
bejeweled by the bodies of youngsters & the hard

clang of real light, & churches, gospel-fat, despite The News.
I think this day will not grow old as I, or you,

& want, forever, its children & magnolias (red kingdom of stoops),
but I watch things die & watch things becoming new

& this adds to the rooms of my heart, another room
for dead day. & the tom-tom of my chest, despite itself, survives

just to live under the racket of cherry blooms
though my recent blood is dangerously gray-eyed. I

move headlong toward the fire of daffodils,
resuscitated by the laughter of birds, & girls.

Noche de Lluvia, San Salvador

Rain who nails the earth,
whose infinite legs
nail the earth, whose silver faces
touch my faces, I marry you. & open
all the windows of my house to hear
your million feral versions
of si si

                  sí

          si

                si

La Boda del Mar y Arena

If we, for long enough, look,
with the clean eyes of children
at what this big house is saying,

we will start to understand
the language of our parents,
what the salt means.

I do not want to marry the wind
who leaves me things the color of gold,
whose tracks mark a serpent round the house.

More, more than parrots, more than gold,
I want my love to know my ear.
My love, I want to know your ear, & in this

instant that is as long as my life, I stand,
rigged with bones, beside the window:
beneath the purple dark of evening coming,

the sea & beach move into each other's mouths
particle by particle; each one wanders
the big rooms of the other.

O, god, let us love
like they love.

A Blooming Tree

Spring is a young guy on his back,
underneath the green, ripe tree
whose small fires we wear
in our hair & on our dresses, the dogwoods
& magnolias, the guy
whose voice is changing
from snow to donkey splay, sprawled out
in his Avirex & doo-rag
in the park I am walking.

      City boy,
you are stiff at first, laid out
flat as a yellow skirt
I dried once on the front lawn,
but then I see you jerk ecstatic, the familiar
funk-bound buck under the air.

& I know.

Spring is your dark tree
between your hands. God bless you
on your back, making flowers
without a woman or a man,
& only the sky to call your husband,
& only the air to suck you clean.

St. Elizabeth

I run high in my body
on the road toward sea.

I fall in love. The things
the wind is telling me.

The yellow sky quiet
in her quiet dress.

Old birds sending news
from the reddish hills.

& the one hawk flying
in the distance overhead.

That hawk is what
the wind says. In love

with the heaving
of my peacock chest,

with my lungs, two wings,
such flying things,

but mine for now, just for now
as I open my stride

above the good, dirt road,
fall in love with the mustard

& coriander dust,
& the far, far mountain

beveled by light, by rain,
the easy eye of the sun, now,

smoke floating across the hillside
like a face I knew once very well.

Very well, I fall in love
with the flowers & the wash

hung like prayer flags, see,
in red Juanita's yard. In love

with the earth the color of earth. In love
with the goats, their bellies & hooves,

& the goat mouths bleating
as they greet me on the road.

I fall in love. How they wear
their strange & double-eyes.

How they do not blink
or laugh at me

or say a thing I understand
when I ask them in my English,

because they circle around my feet,
as if they always *knew* me,

Were you my children once?
Did I know your names?

Oh, little magics?
Little children?

&

& isn't the heart
an ampersand,
magnet between
the seconds of days
& dusks, the peonies
& the fig tree &
the squirrels? Intricate
fist of veins
& muscle, ventricles
& the great aorta. Highway
of loves & years looped
into the record's stutter—
& ampersand.
Greedy mouth,
hungry machine, time
machine. Round & plum-
ish in its parts, beautiful
animal whose limbs
cross strange
as Crazy Legs or
Anne Sexton. &:
a moustache on
the page, dressing the mouth
with a formal hair. Pulling
thing close to every thing,
its blackness
making neighbors
of us all. Dark
like the dark
sign of
infinity
but even more
giving, you remind us
of the heart & how

the heart would
rather die than keep
its two dark arms
all to himself;
his life, like our lives,
depends on what
is at his side.

Ode to the Little "r"

Little propeller
working between
the two fields of my a's,
making my name
a small boat
that leaves the port
of old San Juan
or Ponce,
with my grandfather,
Miguel, on a boat,
or in an airplane,
with a hundred or so
others, leaving the island
for work, cities,
in winters that would break
their bones, make old,
old men out of all of them,
factory workers, domino
players, little islands themselves
who would eat & be eaten by Chicago,
New York, the wars
they fought without
being able to vote for
the president. Little propeller
of their names: Francisco,
Reymundo, Arelis, Margarita,
Hernán, Roberto, Reina.
Little propeller of our names
delivering the cargo of blood
to the streets of Holyoke,
Brooklyn, New London,
Ojai, where the teacher says,
"Say your name?" sweetly,
& the beautiful propeller

working between
the two fields of my a's
& the teacher saying, "Oh!
You mean, 'Are-Raw-Sell-Lease.'"
Or "Robe-Bert-Toe"
or "Marred-Guh-Reetuh, like
the drink!" & the "r"
sounding like a balloon
deflating in the room, sad
& sagging. I am hurt.
It is as if I handed her
all my familiar trees & flowers,
every drawing of the family map
& boats & airplanes & cuatros
& coquis, & she used her English
to make an axe & tried to chop
them down. But, "r," little propeller
of my name, small & beautiful monster
changing shapes, you win. You fly
around the room, little bee, upsetting
the teacher & making all of Class-310A laugh,
you fly over the yard, in our mouths,
as our bodies make airplanes over the grass,
you, little propeller, are taking over the city,
you are the sound of cars racing, the sound
of bicycle spokes fitted with playing cards
to make it sound like we are going fast,
this is our ode to you, little "r," little
machine of our names, simple
as a heart, just working, always,
there when we go to the grocery,
there in the songs
we sing in our sleep.

Running Home, I Saw the Planets

On the way home, going,
with the hill & mammoth clouds
behind me, rushing to the house
before the rain, those beautiful Pakistani girls,
their faces happy as poppies, I thought, those girls
rushing home as I was rushing home
to beat the first small pieces
of rain falling down
like nickels in departing light. There
was the laughing of the beautiful girls,
shrieking gulls, five or six of them (depending
on whether I count myself), the bright
& shining planets of their dresses
lifting, just so, in the wind. & their black hairs.
& the black sound of horses, horses
hoofing it home, the click
& clop of their patent leather hooves—Still, it touches
my ear, this sound. I touch
my heart. I can't stop touching
my heart & saying, Today is my birthday,
you see? For the beautiful clamor of planets
dressed as girls who, running home, have heads.
Whose heads swing black night, running home
on the black feet of horses, from the rain.
Now I understand. Today is my birthday.
It is Thursday, my day. My black day.

iii. a book of graves & birds

Science

We were trying to refind the eye & brain
we had when we were pelicans,

but the wind came down, it had ten hands,
it had more mouths & took & took us far to sea.

The wind was not a fixing wind, not a fixing wind
who painted the door or fed the goats when we were sleeping.

It took us apart with its blue hands, this piece, this piece—
& delivered us to our simultaneous homes.

One home is there! One home is there! It said,
You have been this small before. Though you can't really

remember it, you were not always, always tall,
small, small thing, plural thing—

The Dream

Last night, all night
the dream, the dead
mother, my small sister,
tiny, her mouth
over my shoulder
(screaming) like a knapsack
when she heard the news,
& my brother playing
the stereo. I howled
like the coyotes; myself.
& saw the light outside
below the window, my mother,
young, playing with me
at a rock, in some sunlight
falling over us. I was small.
An old & famous woman
asked her questions:
Who wrote this dream?
I wanted to know.
My brother thought
it was our mother
who wrote it
when she was old.
She did not die, he thought.
But I knew, & called down
to the cotton-head of her then, when
she could not see or hear me.
She would never hear me.
I was not capable of talking
then, yet, & she had died,
after all, & the mother
I call to tell the dream
will not remember, after all
she was not born then, yet,

& needed the first mother to die
before she could use her name
& feed her children.

Self-Portrait as the Snail

Thirty-one.

For years, I am the snail
trailing my thought behind me:
a red horse, or carpet. Royal.
The things I've marked & been marked by,
blood falling behind me like a stranger's tail.
Resourceful Gretel who, in eating all the bread,
lets her blood down to mark the way back home!

Like this:

I carry my meat over the earth's lion mouth
& slowly feed my bodies to the dirt.

Elegy for the Stone

Are you my first sister? Small muscle.
Your gray head flat & dead in my hand.
Your body ran loose, a purple spool of thread
through our mother's Cyclops gate
like a lost tooth or clump of hair.
Now your head rolls like a planet
in my hand. How did you find me here?
Yes, you are my sister.
Very, very much my sister—the black grass
of your hair, inside of which is a head, & inside
your head: the 6 blue suitcases
with the dishes our parents left in Nairobi. How
I carry you now in my pocket, with the other
rocks & shells, small family, rattle of graves,
everywhere, rattle of little lives & graves.

Portrait of the Woman as a Skein

I lost my hands—
        —Erin Molitor

*

Tell me what, on earth,
would make you leave your hands
or want to, at the wash-sink?
in the lemon grove?
on the way home from standing, baffled,
in the grocery?

I have seen you walk into traffic like a bird
with something else on your mind
as though wearing a hat, or a medal from a war.

Sometimes you leave yourself all over.
Sometimes your mind & shoes,
they fall behind you.
Sometimes your body is a skein
unraveling.

Sometimes you carry your heart around like a jar of cats
in heat or crying, I don't remember.

Sometimes, it is true,
you are a church of Catholic schoolgirls.
You knew the hymns once, but forget how they go
so you stand mouthing *hotpotato hotpotato*
in the pews.

So far, the men you love
—or is it you?—

drop jugs of honey in the public streets
on purpose or not on purpose. It is hard to say.

Sometimes your body, in winter, is a dress the snow erases.
Sometimes you are decimated.
Sometimes, still, you remember you are capable of building
          houses.

Sometimes, it is true, you are like Lake Sovetskaya.
Buried underneath an arctic ice sheet:

_____

(   ).

You think this might be safer.
With everything & nothing ajar.

                    *

Private, mysterious Perhaps, Dear Friend,
landscape of potential bedazzlements gleaming
like ice-skate blades at the Mojave Desert Salvation Army.
You are suitable & unsuitable.
All the songs you know are from a different country.
The fruits in your father's poems
do not grow here.

You have lost the turquoise jacket
with your name magic-markered inside.

Your face is cold.

Your hands are cold.

Sometimes you leave your hair at the bus station
& get on the bus.

Sometimes you leave your hair at the bus station
& get on the bus & as your face falls asleep against the window
you realize it is all your body now, everything between you
& the pieces you lost once, the towers & crows,
the city (you) gleaming
in long, glorious hyphen
beneath stars.

Sometimes you are a broken barn.
Sometimes you are the street & trees.
Sometimes a spool of purple string.

You are a colander, sometimes
losing things.

Sometimes what keeps you alive is a mystery.

                          *

Last night, the dream of you standing
in the doorway like a lighthouse
calling for your hands to come back
home, & from a great distance, them
running towards you, two
children or two dogs. What scared you then,
you also called it beautiful—
the way their breath flew out of them like clouds,
the way they reached the dark yard panting & stood
deciding between the body & the woods.

Three Girls, One of Them a Coward Girl

The great & eerie lake
of this memory seeps
through the trees, in the pail,
through the house, away

from us—they dashed & turned.
We have never been cats before,
but pretend we are their mothers
that afternoon, we fill the garbage pail

with water from the garden hose
as the neighbor-girl skates the blank
face of her sad & clean yard
where nothing grows.

We are busy drowning cats, though
we say we are saving them &
making them clean, so drop
the small mouths into water & scream,

the way they thrash before we reach
(I do not) back into the pail to save them,
away from the clear, gray eye of the human
mother who would stop our game forever

if she saw. We were hunters.
To see them scatter, frantic,
made our teeth grow long.
300 years after the fact, I could write

six sentences about cruelty
& what it means to build a trap,
but I am most afraid of how quickly we said
"yes," & "yes" again, to the bright confusion

of their bodies in water, how frightened
the hand from reaching into that mess
of fangs & leaping eyes, how frightened
of saving them. I wish

I were a hero. That type, who
despite the bite, knew,
what to do. & did it. Or
the neighbor girl, far away

from the rest of us in this memory now,
on her roller skates, back & forth, as if
silently countering the death we conjured
by filling her sad yard with the shadow & skin

of her moving, living body
over the lot, her body
killing nothing
with its hands.

Self-Portrait as the Snake

Silver snake slinking through the grandmother
yard, on my belly, without speech.
No one sees me, but the boy,

the boy is fat & beautiful
& he sits on the counter like a cake.
Outside my grandmother snaps

the neck of the chive with her hands.
It is my cousin. Long & thin,
the both of us, & the centipedes

& pinchers who blindly waved
their bodies at me
when I had hands & lifted

bricks in the garden. Back then,
like them, when the light touched me
I wanted to stand & hallelujah,

& I wanted to run away. Now,
the garden is a skin I wear. Somewhere
in the box of this old house,

my child-skin hangs quietly between the coats,
shed: a parachute or bag full of red dirt & teeth.
Inside the child-skin are 6 men from Adis Ogdo

drinking boon beneath a giant tree they've carried with them
into the skin, fat & loaded now, with boon & Jalisco
accordionists, their sad songs kill me, oh,

I am older now, but not old. I am looking back
to when I was a girl; now my body's a flash
of poison on the floor. The weather of the house,

it shapes the body's light. This is what
a girl has in common with the lightning.

Self-Portrait as the Airplane
(Ode to the Noise in the Ear)

I was 7, an airplane
in the Aliso Viejo public pool.
The way I moved, face down
& slowly in the turquoise blue, gliding
from end to end, delivering my brother
to the concrete banks.
I was an airplane & felt deaf
like Uncle Nino who sound entered spangled
& warbling. Inside of his ear was a hearing aid.
He placed it in my ear once,
as though putting a small nest
in the rafters of a dollhouse,
a small, pink-colored suitcase of sounds
like a tiny glee-egg back into the rafters
of a house. Tiniest sadness
inside the ear, how I held it in my body, carefully,
not wanting the ear to blink or swallow
the small gravestone I tried on
like a prosthetic limb. I did not want
to but was more sad to say no. Instead,
stood still & felt the small thing tell me
about the body's first death below the laughs
& ordinary sounds clanging like miracles
from down the hall, exaggerated, in the red room,
I swear I could hear my grandmother
whispering with my aunt, I can't remember
what they said, but I thought
about a doctor's stethoscope,
& what is the sound of that one big kid, perpetually jumping
feet first into the deep side
of a pool's blue rectangle,
the silence & plunge, dispersal
of plates through the body's dark rooms

as my brother & I took turns shouting
each other's names underwater
& the kid made booms & booms? Canon ball.
Every thing was vanishing or about
to vanish, & we sharpened our ears like knives,
glad for how they worked.
I am greedy, greedy, greedy for the sound of gravel
under truck-tires, crickets, distant
soprano scratch of airplane
against the sky. My ears eat & eat.
All day. In sleep.
Like sitting down to a meal
without kissing my hands,
I am the angel of nothing.
If these ears were birds, I'd like for them to be
flying birds. But the ears are bodies,
they do what they want. Somewhere a hammer
echoes against a nail-point entering wood. Write it down.
The ear is not a jukebox, it opens its mouth & swallows
jackhammers, coyotes, & the tambourines, god,
give me the good & common sense
to keep the tongue from cursing
at this news.

Central City Senior Center, New Orleans

for Ellen, after Jane Kenyon

It'll probably be, old friend,
that we won't be there
to witness the last breath, one
for the other, but, oh,
there were hours spent
following a brass band
through the Trémè, stomps
caught in a tree of horns
& shadows over the dry, black streets
& the *tak-tak* of the cowbell
in a big man's hand. & that time
we stood at the sea, bodies lit
by the giant, yellow O.
Old friend, I knew
you were something special
when we danced at the Senior Center
that time with Carla & David, & the old,
pretty lady got up & did a slow wind behind
the dance teacher's back & I said to you,
"That's you." & you said,
"That's right it is."
& how when we left
there was a white-haired lady,
funny in the parking lot,
feeding pigeons with the bread
from her fanny pack, in front
of a big truck she paid no attention to
though it was waiting for her to move
& my eyes caught a flood & I turned
looking for someone who would understand
I'd just seen my angel
throwing bread down to the pigeons

just kindly, slowly. & you, without my saying
a thing, as if you heard the chest its joy
& cardinal, you said *yeah*, just that.
How marvelous. Ordinary. To get to see
& turn around, & know somebody else
was seeing, too. One day it will be
otherwise. I always meant to thank you
for that. Thank you. What is close to my heart
is that woman, that city, you, that noon
on the dry land dressed in pigeons & daylight,
the dry land dressed in our brief lives, our lives
brief & miraculous, as the bees.

Self-Portrait as the Pirate's Gold

When I was 8 or 10
my mouth made
an odd x-ray:

> a third front tooth
> inside   the gum
> lodged   like the lintel
> of   a door.

They must have made
a pretty family,
those permanents, though,
in sleep the dentists took
that treasure, extraction
of my third front tooth,
like gold or an egg, my loot.

Strange to throw the body in the trash.
I am intimate with the crows & rats.

Self-Portrait as the Snake's Skin

elegy for a rooster

This morning I sneak out of your bed,
& am the red skin of the snake who leaves
the thick meat of your muscle.

In other words, I take my skin,
a costume, to the kitchen,
& stand in the white air
of the women you wore,
the smell of their furs
nailed to the wall
in taxiderm.

      Once,
you roamed so far towards other pink
that my face crossed the road
when it saw you coming.
      Cock-a, Cock-a,
      I am a chicken. & could not
turn away,
you were mine.
      Your animal hand
      has axed
      my sense
      again,
      & I opened my dress
      to let you climb in
      to where I am
      a photo-booth.
      For free,
      my god blinked
      light in flashes
      around you

while you danced,
my brain sang
funeral songs.

Now you're breathing like farm
in the other room
& the lintel between us
is a guillotine.

I'll miss you, deer,
but I choose my head
& carry it out of doors:
a bucket of eels
to set loose
in the dark, December sea.

To the Husband

Not unlike a zoo, with hammers & nails,
you shoved me into rooms & bathrooms
& told me to sing, sing, until I, like a (l)I(on)
snapped my gold jaw around your khaki-man shoulder.

Now say it's hot out. & you're in a city like Anaheim
or Honolulu, & the glint of the sun against car-chrome or ocean's
a soprano pitch you almost understand, you don't know why, &
it makes you take your shirt off & a little girl points to the teeth

marks, What is that? & you'd almost forgotten the lion at home.
Say you tell her Nothing, but she can smell her mother's bite
on your skin & nothing begins to grow inside her, a vague
atmosphere slowly erasing the organists who played, back, forth,

in her rooms & chest, songs about god. God. I was a girl once,
I moved in thin line, out & in doors, my sex rolled up
like a discarded fence or carpet, red, I found at a junkyard, or
a guillotined head, rescued from the dumpster-bin. Poinsettia,

the pet mice; all the time useful, beautiful lives discarded. How
do you see something dying & beg for it to get its song back?
My own girl is giving up her teeth. She hangs them from her ears.
This is not what I wanted her to do with the story. The thing

I was saying about the junkyard & my sex, I meant for it
to be a quilt about resuscitation. I never set the house on fire.
I never killed the doors & spoons. I wanted every thing to live.
In my sleep, I give my children hands & they go back to swing

open the aviaries of the old neighborhood. Mostly, I want them
to see the birds of their own bodies through the window.
What was wild in them, I want for them to see it. & remember.
The feral howl of laughing as they threw their skins down

among the leaves. A lucky woman gets to see her children dance
eagle in the yard, arms out in a carnival of feathers
like the old folks used to be in Griffith. Kicking up dust.
The body, with its arms up, is a kind of miracle—translating light

& news between the realms—It is science.
The science quails our marrow with eagles & laughing.
On top of our house, like a bird, it sings, *Husband,*
this, youcouldnotkill, youcouldnotkill.

This Morning the Small Bird Brought a Message from the Other Side

I would not call it fear
or the absence of fear
that I woke with, but worry,
this morning when I rose
up from the bed, & saw,
with clear seeing, for the first time,
that my chest was a small, red cup,
or bird in my hand, somehow
thirsty, its injury
made me panic for it
& I carried it with me
not knowing what to do
with its small speech, the way
　　　　　it said your name.

I want to know what to do
with the dead things we carry.

If I were to wake
another morning,
maybe tomorrow,
with the red thing in my chest
or hand, what would
I do? Will I?

& the bird, would it attempt,
to cross over, would it come again
from the body's realm
of animals & claws?
Would it risk its life
again to give me the message
of your name?

Would I trust my mouth
to resuscitate the messenger, small bird,
knowing I could kill it
with my teeth?

iv. a book of erased cities

Elegy in Gold

Earring, tooth,
dog breath, shoe,

mango fruit or pocket watch,
sunlight on my love's

elbow, sunlight
in the kettle's steam,

we walk in the rubble
of the African dream

brushing shipwreck from
our hair & dresses.

This is the country
of the gone-away: Harlem,

you wear the missing
like a golden chain.

They Tell Me You Are Gone

All day long the birds shout *Phebus! Phebus!*
& the geese, if I didn't know better,
would sound like donkeys. & they do.
& somewhere, a girl loves a boy with her dark hand,
& we come upon them in the park
where the walkway is so skinny
that my dress-hem catches fire
when we pass. & just like that,
my mother chopping onions far away
sees a volcano at the kitchen table
& puts the knife down to call,
& the telephone rings, but I am out
without it, & rings, & the day goes on howling
through the branches, over the giant park-green
going up & down. & the boy losing his mind.

I am dying, or you. & the crow-headed women
running in the distance
from some devil or dog, I think,
over such grass in my eye.

& one by one, or two at a time,
something invisible snatches them up
by the black tumbleweed of their hair. & this
would be a myth, except it's not.

& to think, just this morning, I was one of them
walking out of my house
into the day's shrike brain.

All day long, someone is yanked
up into the sky or down into the mulch
or in his bed or trampled or headfirst,
face down, with or without the news.

& all day long, people going in & out
of each other, their houses, the supermarket.
Dying & coming & shopping for tomatoes
maybe at the same time. & to think,
people burn like this, simultaneously, in kitchens & beds,
the heady dusk of the public park
while children are learning songs. Oh, hair,
was the sky always so blue
as it is now, taking the jet-black & sequoia of our girls?
Every thing taking another thing home to bed
for one night or two nights
or, not even a night, or 600 days,
which is to say, *Lifeguard, drop the whistle.*
Mother, turn out the lights on your front-porch—
one day your girl will not come back. They tell me
you are gone, & all day long, the day goes on
bucking logic into the hills. How the geese dress the dusk
in donkey-call. How the sixteen stars keep time
as our bodies, in their different sleeps, are rearranged,
& we wake up wearing each other's clothes:
spider wearing my mouth like a room,
& the good black ant carries your small material,
some fleck of sugar hidden
in the silver back room of your tooth, off
like a peony or a bone, & there you go.

        All day long the wind wears Phebus' shoes.
        I want to live longer knowing this.

The Doorway of Our Mother's Leg Leads Me to You, Brother

In the food section of the swap meet,
all of us standing & eating like horses. Hot dogs,
the nervous laughing of teenagers, & the far away face
of the woman whose skin moved,
ruddy, beneath a screen of smoke. Our mother's leg
in spasms, having just come up from the wheelchair of her surgery.
The nerves gone rogue, haywire, split into two,
one side over there & one side over there, her leg
convulsing with the argument. That's just how it was.
I wish I could remember what we did with our faces. All I see
is our mother's, the shame & branding of the muscle's buck
whipped red by the nerves' quick revolt. I see her face.
Always coming & going from school, I barely knew the routine.
How long it would last. Our aunt, our cousins, & the baby.
But most of all, you, Brother. I wish I never left.
The year turned without our ever paying attention,
& not when the calendar said it would. One day,
we looked up & everything was different. The mail comes.
Yours in your name, mine in my name. Now,
two different sides of the country & your hair
is turning. The death that cuts me most is the one I never say
out loud. I am leaving for boarding school,
the rental van is packed. You are not
coming with me for the first real time.
This story is an axe when the van
pulls away. Distance is fat & bleeds, marks the second
death. But, you see, the heart still works. It is almost unbearable—
the heart that works. It must know something
my head doesn't know.

Mrs. S

I have been put down like a horse
with a bad leg, no good for running
or pulling a cart of fruit. Brute,
this body of ridiculous, haphazard trees.
I was a bell once, I was
a teacher who raised my hand into the air
on the schoolyard & the children knew to stand in a line
though the sky was blue. My body
stacked itself up & up. Each
small part lifted another part high,
until my hand was taller than
my head. It was the tallest I'd ever be.
Now, beneath the grass & daisies:
my body is thin, a yellowed horizon. I am not asleep.
I am not asleep. The tumor in my breast,
whose nest? Beneath the dark & chewing dirt,
I miss the song of the purple plum, I want
one thousand days of sun.

People, I heard the news the other day
like to scare me half to death...
TV say a spaceship is comin here
if it do wont be no people left

But I tell you folks, spaceship cant be so bad...
I been on earth all my life,
and all my life I been mad...
—Henry Dumas, "Outer Space Blues"

Night, for Henry Dumas

Henry Dumas, 1934–1968
did not die by a spaceship
or flying saucer or outer space at all
but was shot down, at 33,
by a New York City Transit policeman
will be shot down, May 23rd,
coming home, in just 6 days, by a New York City Transit
        policeman
in the subway station singing & thinking of a poem,
what he's about to eat, will be, was, is right now
shot down, this sad conjugation,
happening yesterday, happened tomorrow,
will happen now
under the ground & above the ground
at Lenox & 125th in Harlem, Tennessee,
Memphis, New York, Watts, Queens.
1157 Wheeler Avenue, San Quentin, above which
sky swings down a giant rope, says
Climb me into heaven, or follow me home,
& Henry
& Amadou
& Malcolm
& Oscar
& Sean

& King,
& the night hangs over the men & their faces,
& the night grows thick above the streets,
I swear it is more blue, more black, tonight
with the men going up there.
Bring the children out
to see who their uncles are.

Break

When the boys are carnivals
we gather round them in the dark room
& they make their noise while drums
ricochet against their bodies & thin air
below the white ceiling hung up like a moon
& it is California, the desert. I am driving in a car,
clapping my hands for the beautiful windmills,
one of whom is my brother, spinning,
on a hillside in the garage
with other boys he'll grow old with, throw back.
How they throw back their bodies
on the cardboard floor, then spring-to, flying
like the heads of hammers hitting strings
inside of a piano.
               Again, again.
This is how they fall & get back up. One
who was thrown out by his father. One
who carries death with him like a balloon
tied to his wrist. One whose heart will break.
One whose grandmother will forget his name.
One whose eye will close. One who stood
beside his mother in a green hospital. One
kick up against the air to touch the earth.
See him. Fall. Then get back up.

English Class

for Anthony

Like the first time I ever saw a cardinal,
brilliant flash of red against the gray
of the English room, your voice clapped
against the windows; signal: fireflies in the blood.

Whispered: the hieroglyphics of ancient Egyptians,
into your dream of subway cars threading language,
Technicolor, through the dark eyes of a vanishing city
your mother & uncles tended, like a garden, in their stories.

Little Arachne, little spider weaving realms, we hear you
filling your poems with mirrors & with tongues. & now
you're filling your poems with guns. Blood.
Even when I tell you, Anthony, to write about the trees

you only remember what part of the world is an axe,
the murder the hands are capable of. I used to hope to run
from this. I used to worry, worry. Since
I met you I've been remembering the story of salt. Lot's wife.

But you tell me something the story never did:
Look back at the burning city. Still, live.

Mississippi Burial, On the Ferry to Algiers

New Orleans

Not loose, the belly after catfish,
though the trombone throws a hook
in your waters, makes you move
under the lights' heat, the horn's loud ink
now a set of arms, now a membrane of music
you wear through the rooms & streets
of The Quarter beneath ghosts
who walk beside you telling things:
their names, the color of their hair & children.
They say
>*Violet*
>*Rebekkah*
>*Au Lait*
>*Crow*

Now they tell you about the water
from Algiers to Canal Street, it's
hundreds of feet deep. If you buried
all the women standing, the killed women,
kept women, women loved & unloved
who lost something important to this
river Mississippi, if you buried them standing
on one another's shoulders, from the bottom of the silty bed,
they would rise higher than the water, than the buildings.
The raucous of their skin & feathers are not seen by every eye,
but sometimes a woman will look you in the face
& say the name your grandmother was called. I mean,
it is possible to wear your ghosts like a face,
which is to say, my face has been here before.
Your talk. The heart is a fist of windows & church-bells
from 1852. The pigeons then are the pigeons now.
The cats crying "hello" at the window. Somewhere,
on a street in Algiers my heart is breaking, still,

though the highway marks time, says Whole days
are passing, sometimes the breaking thing
is perpetual. Mother, where is your son?
What will you do, husband, when your wife has been sold?
Husband, what will you do when your wife has been sold
for coins, to a plantation owner of things, the rest of the country
standing wide-eyed at the TV?
& the river said,

> *Holy are the good.*
> *Holy are the lovers.*
> *Holy the crawfish, catfish*
> *going about their business*
> *not taking more than they need.*

Genius-holy, the glow of the quiet work
of fish beneath the water,
like prayer—that slither down in the murky guts
of the river, humming with the noise
of fish, fish praying all through the water,
piece by piece, & with their mouths,
delivering, into another life,
the big & drowning cities of women & land
say,

> *Sing me a song when you cross this river*
> *& let that song be a burial song.*
>
> *If it is true, how they say it,*
> *that we only pass on once,*
>
> *then I will wait here, in the river,*
> *for my burial song. Make it be*
>
> *a good song. Something that will help*
> *me to get up & cross over to the other side.*
>
> *Make it be a good song*
> *& dress it with feathers & beads.*

Make it last a thousand years
& come & sing it to me, you all,

one by one, so my death life
lasts longer than my living one.

I want to be the one
with the longest funeral.

Let the song you sing
be a burial song.
Fill it, please, with horns
& shells. Let it go on

for days & days, so that my burial song
lasts longer than my living one.

Explaining the Land Mine to the Small Child

Weapon, shrapnel,
like uncontrollable fire,
like knives,
angry sun, killer
of everything.

What words, anyway, can
be used to warn the children
when no word is as terrible
as the hand & the mine?
What words, anyway, can
be used to warn the children
who sing so beautifully
the names of their favorite friends,
of the heart & the moon,
to the roosters in the yard?

To Waste My Hands

Three years ago, I stood on the dock near my father's house
while the small shark suffocated & was killed.

He was like an angel culled up from the purple sea.
& the air smashed into him like an anvil

& his muscles sank desperately into the ribs. Terrible

terrible, terrible, terrible, terrible, terrible, terrible
to watch him that way. More terrible to waste my hands, just
       standing.

Praise Song for the Donkey

*for Lama & Haya & the donkey, killed by an Israeli missile
in Beit Lahiya, northern Gaza*

*"It was not possible to identify which parts belonged to the
donkey & the girls."*
                    —Witness, Gaza, Palestine, 2009.

Praise the Mohawk roof
of the donkey's good & gray head, praise
its dangerous mane hollering out. Beneath
her soft & mournful gray, still beneath
the skull, where it is dusk, praise
the rooms of the donkey's eye & brain,
its pulley & clang, this sound
of hooves & the girls still saying words.
Praise the girls still saying words,
praise the girls, their hands, the hooves
of their hearts hoofing against their opened chests
opened on the open road plainly, praise
the plain day, praise the donkey in it, praise
the fat tongue's memory of grass or hay,
the hundred nights of animal sleep
flung far from bodies, the sturdy houses of bones, all over
the decimated road where every thing is flying, praise
the deep, dark machine of the donkey's eye,
the girl's eye, like a movie-house crumbling
in a field outside of town—,
praise the houses & rocks it held once, the sky
before & after the missile, praise the dark
& donkey soul crossing over, every one,
every hill & girl it ever saw, crossing over
in the red suitcase of its blood, into the earth,
praise the donkey earth, earth of girls,
earth of funerals & girls, praise the small,

black luggage of the donkey's eye
in a field, flung far,
filling the ants & birds
with what
it saw.

I Am Not Ready to Die Yet

after Joy Harjo

I am not ready to die yet: magnolia tree
going wild outside my kitchen window
& the dog needs a house, &, by the way,
I just met you, my sisters & I
have things to do, & I need
to talk on the phone with my brother. Plant a tree.
& all the things I said I'd get better at.

In other words, I am not ready to die yet
because didn't we say we'd have a picnic
the first hot day, I mean,
the first really, really hot day?
Taqueria. & swim, kin,
& mussel & friend, don't you go, go, no.

Today we saw the dead bird, & stopped for it.
& the airplanes glided above us. & the wind
lifted the dead bird's feathers.

I am not ready to die yet.
I want to live longer knowing that wind
still moves a dead bird's feathers.
Wind doesn't move over & say *That thing*
can't fly. Don't go there. It's dead.
No, it just blows & blows lifting
what it can. I am not ready
to die yet. No.

I want to live longer.
I want to love you longer, say it again,
I want to love you longer
& sing that song

again. & get pummeled by the sea
& come up breathing & hot sun
& those walks & those kids
& hard laugh, clap your hands.
I am not ready to die yet.

Give me more dreams. To taste the fig.
To hear the coyote, closer.
I am not ready to die yet.
But when I go, I'll go knowing
there will be a next time. I want

to be like the cactus fields
I drove through in Arizona.
If I am a cactus, be the cactus
I grow next to, arms up,
every day, let me face you,
every day of my cactus life.

& when I go or you go,
let me see you again somewhere,
or you see me.

Isn't that you, old friend, my love?
you might say, while swimming in some ocean
to the small fish at your ankle.
Or, *Weren't you my sister once?*
I might say to the sad, brown dog who follows me down
the street. Or to the small boy
or old woman or horse eye
or to the tree. *I know I knew I know you, too.*
I'm saying, could this be what makes me stop
in front of *that* dogwood, train whistle, *those* curtains
blowing in that window. See now,
there go some eyes you knew once
riding the legs of another animal,
wearing its blue sky, magnolia,

wearing its bear or fine
or wolf-wolf suit, see,
somewhere in the night a mouth is singing
You remind me   You remind me
& the heart flips over in the dusky sea of its chest
like a fish signaling *Yes, yes it was me!*
&, yes, it was, & you were there, & are here now,
yes, honey, yes hive, yes I will, Jack,
see you again, even if it's a lie, don't
let me know, not yet, not ever, I need to think
I'll see you, oh,
see you
again.

& When We Woke

It rained all night. It did not rain.
I strapped my life to a buoy—& sent it out.
& was hoping for a city whose citizens sing
from their windows or rooftops,
about the beauty of their children
& their children's eyes, & the color of the fields
when it is dusk. & was hoping for a city
as free as the rain, whose people roam
wherever they want, free as any real, free thing is free.
Joyful. Green. & was hoping
for a city of 100 old women whose bones
are thick & big in their worker hands
beautiful as old doors. & when we woke,
dear reader, we'd landed in a city of 100 old women
telling their daughters things. & when we turned
to walk away, because we did not think we were citizens
of this strange & holy place, you & I, the hundred old
women said, *No, No! You are one of us! We are your*
mothers! You! You! Too! Come & listen to our secrets.
We are telling every person with a face!
& they stood us in a line facing the sea,
(because that is the direction we came from)
& behind us there was another line of women
& another, & we sang songs. & we filled the songs
with our mothers' names. & we filled the songs
with trees for our mothers to stand under,
& good water for our mothers to drink. & we filled
the songs with beds for our mothers to lay down in
& rest. We filled the songs with rest. & good food
for our mothers to eat. We made them a place
in our singing, & we faced the sea.
We are still making them a place
in our singing. Do you understand?
We make them a place where they can walk freely,

untouched by knives or the police who patrol
the borders of countries like little & fake hatred-gods
who patrol the land though the land says, *I go on*
& on, so far, you lose your eye on me.
We make our mothers a place in our singing & our place
does not have a flag or, even, one language.
Do you understand? We sing like this for days,
standing in lines & lines & lines, facing the sea.
The sea knows what to do. We sing like this for days
until our throats are torn with singing. Do you understand?
We must build houses for our mothers in our poems. I am not sure,
but think, This is my wisest song.

On Kindness

after Nazim Hikmet, for & after Rassan

At the Detroit Metro Airport
with the turtle-hours to spare
between now & my flight, there is
such a thing as the kindness
of the conveyor belt who lends me
its slow, strange mollusk foot
as I stand quiet, exhausted, having been
alone in my bed for days now, sleeping
in hotels, having spent months, now,
without seeing the faces of my family, somehow
its slow & quiet carrying of the load
reminds me of the kindness of donkeys,
& this kindness returns me to myself.
It reminds me of the kindness of other things I love
like the kindness of sisters who send mail,
wherever you are, &, speaking of mail, there is
the special kindness of the mail lady
who says, "Hi, baby" to everyone, at first
I thought it was just to me, but now I know
she says "Hi, baby" to everyone. That is kindness.
Too, there is the kindness of windows, & of dogs.
& then there was that extraordinary Sunday
back at the house, I heard a woman screaming
about how she was lonely & so lonely
she didn't know what she'd do, maybe kill
herself, she said, over & over like a parrot
in a cage, a parrot whose human parent
only taught it that one sentence. I looked out
the window & saw her from behind, the way she flung
her arms like she was desperate & being killed
or eaten by an invisible predator, like a tiger or a lion, in the chest.
& her voice seemed fogged out with methadone, I don't know,

something, & I walked away from the window
& sat, angry with her for screaming, & sad,
& not long after, I heard her saying,
What'd you say? What'd you say to me?
& a man's voice, low, I could not tell if it was kind.
& she said, *I'll kill myself, I'm so lonely.*
& did I tell you, yet, that it was Mother's Day?
Flowers & mothers, flowers & mothers all day long.
& the woman saying, *I'm so lonely. I could kill myself.*
& then quiet. & the man's voice saying, *It's okay.*
It's okay. I love you, it's okay.

& this made me get up, put my face, again, to the window
to see my landlord's nephew outside, just hugging her so, as if
it were his mother, I mean, as if he belonged to her,
& then, again, quiet, I left the window but sat
in the silence of the house, hidden by shutters, & was amazed.
When the front door of the brownstone opened up
& let the tall nephew in with his sad & cougar eyes,
handsome & tall in his Carolina-Brooklyn swagger, I heard
him start to climb the stairs above me, & my own hand
opened up my own front door,
& though it was none of my business
I asked him, *Do you know that woman out there?*
& do you know what happened next?
He said, *No.* The nephew said no, he didn't know
the woman out there. & he told me Happy Mother's Day
as he climbed the rest of the stairs. & I can't stop seeing them
hugging on the street, under trees, it was spring, but cold,
& sometimes in the memory his head is touching hers
& sometimes in the memory his eyes are closed,
& sometimes she is holding him
& singing to him *I love you. It's okay.*
I mean to tell you that everywhere I go
I hear us singing to each other. This way. I mean to tell you
that I have witnessed such great kindnesses as this,
in this, my true life, you must believe me.

I mean, on a Sunday, when nobody was supposed to be
watching. Nobody at all. I saw this happen, the two
of them hugging, when nobody was supposed to be
watching, but not a secret either, public
as the street, not for glory & not for a joke,
the landlord's nephew ready to stand there for the woman
like a brother or a sister or a husband or son,
or none of those at all, but a stranger,
a stranger who, like her, is an earthling.
Perhaps this thing I am calling kindness
is more simple than kindness, rather, recognition
of the neighbor & the blue, shared earth
& the common circumstance of being here:
what remains living of the last
two million, impossible years...

v. a fable

On the Shape of the Sentence

for S

She is my she.

~~Begin here: She.~~
~~No. Begin again: Sh.~~

Begin:

S

The snake. Not the symbol of the snake but the snake itself.
Two headed, two tailed, one of each, whatever.
The curl of wisdom, temptation.

The silty daughter, grandchild, extra finger, friend—pulls the fruit
from the tree or barrel because the snake has told her so.
There is some knowledge there. What did the snake say
according to Bible? Said Holy Book?   "fhsjlhfuos"
But probably the snake had a lisp & said:
          sthere isth sthome sthknowledge sthere
          sthat sthyou sthmight sthwant.

She takes it. Took it. Will take it. No one has forced her. She cannot
know what it will do to her mouth, heart, eyes, eyebrows—to taste it.
Call it starfruit, sex, apple, cocaine, x, whatever. Does she take it? Yes.
She takes it. It tastes good to her. It tastes good to her. It tastes good
to her.

This is the before   **S**   after:
          it is a playground slide.
          it is a roller coaster, boomerang.
          it spits her out into a silence.

Sh: the thing, the way she loves

it.

She would like it again, again.

Per-

haps it provides her respite

from:

> Adam
> her mother
> the earth
> Choose one. No, let us
> move away from that
> kind of guessing.

Sh: Imagine she is on her own—impossible—but relatively on her own
      in the world.
A thin line dragging itself through doors, in & out of rooms, work, onto
      buses
& trains. She is developing a city of desire. Building herself into a house
      of stories,

      3rd story   [potholders, phone numbers, red telephone,
materials]
     2nd story   [photographs, handkerchiefs, cameras, pans, a wolf?]
1st story   [rugs, carpets, books, dishes]

      3rd story   [*I was born with eight eyes, she says.*]
     2nd story   [*The tree in the back of the house is, actually, the grandmother.*]
1st story   [*Nothing mattered anyway.*]

She stacks herself & fills herself like this. She fills the stories, the house
with objects, flowers. Sometimes she cleans the rooms, folds the cold
clothes, sometimes not. She fills the cupboards with the s(h)ilent thing
& carries it around with her like an extra limb she has grown. Mostly she
is aSHamed of it. Mostly she gets to the gym early, or the public pool,
& if she is interrupted by other early-goers who are hiding their extra
limbs (some of them) & not hiding their extra limbs (some of them), she

pulls the fire alarm so that everyone will be distracted when she scurries
out dragging her silence like a tail or a third foot despite the beautiful &
polka-dotted bikini.

Begin again.

S is the aerial view of the girl standing with one arm in front of her. It is
her left arm in front of her. It is clutching daffodils, her right arm behind
her is holding the sound 'Sh.' She does not think we can see it. From
here, we can see it.

S is the line we make, chasing her. We would like her to show us what is
in her right hand. We would like to see the Sh & what it is. S is the line
we make, chasing her through the ruins of the garden. We are trying to
know what she will do with the sh.

S is the girl sitting, head hung down.
Dolorous, the shape. Perhaps
she is kneeling. Perhaps she
has lost her hands & she is kneeling
in the grass
trying to find them.

&, girl, where would they go if they could run away from you?
What are your hands most hungry for?
Tell us, what caused this severance?
Did the rest of you mistrust the hands?
Or did the hands mistrust the bigger body,
the bully head?

She hears these questions & cannot decide if she is asking them or if they
belong to something else.

She:

What would turn the curve of the S into the embryonic: e?
Evolution in words, in the progression of the line as it travels through the
sentence.

Left to right. Up to down. Right to left. & so on. Does it matter where it started & which way it moves? Or does it only matter that it started once? & that, yes, it moves. Evolves. Shapeshifts. & changes. What does the shapeshifting of the line tell us about the girl in question?

S: she was a blooming, wild line once. Spinning. Happening. Actual. The flowers, remember, in her hand—& behind her back, the quiet thing.

Sh: & then the things that caused her silence: a house full of boxes, everything wrapped. How will the girl know what is real & not real? The true color of her mother's hair? The earth is a face far, far from her.

e: even the dragonfly returns to its once-stillness. This is the shape she made in the sonogram. The word ends where she began, once: folded, bowing, almost recognizable.

She: is.

i

> young, little Cyclops
> the stalk-thin body & the eye
> one-eyed i
> little girl, black line, black eye, black i.

is

little Cyclops, one-eyed i, not yet I.
not yet a scarecrow standing in a field of lilies (white),
she is little, little, little, but the essential thing has been born,
the one small eye goes everywhere she goes,
intractable as her bones, the fact of her
at all.

is

little Cyclops, you are, again, a praying thing,
not mantis, but a human animal, what did it take

to make you kneel down, so? where did your eye go
when you bowed, snakely, to the grass?

She is "m," but not m. More, she is:
> two hills,
> mountainous, somehow, in her vastness,
> some ride, roller coaster,
> what is left of her route are footsteps marking
> descent, ascent, descent, ascent, descent again
> What does she smell in that underworld
> & who does she see? The dream tells me
> she took bread with her & went down looking
> for her cousin, hoping he would walk out
> from the deep, dark crevice of his death
> & tell her something. The bread, she meant
> to feed him some, or mark her way so as to know
> the direction of the door she first walked through,
> but the plan failed, she got lost anyway, & was thirsty
> until the water diviner ('y'), in the middle of the road,
> told her where the water was & where she might find
> the thing she needed most: someone who knew her
> name or would claim her, no matter.

She is my: In the map of this sentence which is, more or less, her map.
(What did it mean when people said things like "more or less"?) In the
map of this sentence (which is her map) the Cyclops is not unlike a series
of hills & she is a water diviner, or a young girl with both her hands up
not singing hallelujah but offering to be some kind of weathervane, a
thing for lightning to move through when she is out on her bicycle or
walking to the store. At any given moment she throws her hands up &
offers for something to take her. It never takes her quickly, rather, the
wind slowly eats her as it eats each of us. Slowly, slowly, quiet as a fish.
It takes small pieces of her into its mouth, small fish, sucking the tiniest
particle of her skin into itself. One day sh(w)e will end up in the bellies
of fishes. To this, she throws her hands up again, but this time it strikes
her down:
> s

What to do with another s? Another little girl kneeling with her hands in the grass, trying to find something. But, no. This s has been struck down. By lightning. By the knowledge that one day (we all, we all) will find ourselves to be little Jonahs. Little Jonahs in the middle of the fishes' bellies. Or the bright, blue earth—a Jonah, too, in the deep, starred belly of space. What, possibly, could resuscitate the girl? Or has she gone, now, too soon. Too soon into the belly of the grass or whale?

The birds say things above her! They are making a fuss!
The birds say, *Call the three wise aunts!*

& then the camels & ostriches, standing court, in the front yard. The sages look at the shape her body makes in the grass:

s

One wise aunt says, *She is showing us we have always been the snake, same-shaped.*

No, the second aunt says. *She is just sleeping. She doesn't know the line her body makes in the grass. Her eyes are not far enough away from her, anyway, to see it.*

& the third aunt is quiet. & says nothing.

No, says the girl, suddenly, startling the aunts (all of them) with the clear articulation.

I have buried the things we lost. I took their names away & gave their bodies back. I took their names away so they would go.

The first aunt, observing what is obvious, says, *Not a fit at all, but a funeral.*

sh, she says, I do not want them to mistake our talking for their last song. *sh, 'til they are gone*, she says, sh, *'til they are gone.*

& the aunts wait until all of the going is done. & then they leave her, too.

& she stands in the clean air herself, cleaned & licked by mourning who licked her face & hands with its wolf mouth & tongue.

She is my sh, she says suddenly aware of the sentence. & the wolf lumbers away without her, sensing, in the girl, the absence of fear.

The absence of fear makes the wolf
mistake the girl, herself, for wolf
& so she doesn't eat her with her teeth.
She lumbers away.

She is my sh, & everything is quiet.

But what would turn the quiet into anything else? Into a painting? Or noise again? The girl turns, now, & walks away, far from the graves. Far from the graves. Farther still.

Her cloven feet mark the earth with the strange flowers of her tracks: e
e   e   e

& she walks like that for years, alone like that, until she comes upon a mirror. *Who are you? Who are you?* the girl asks.

Is my. Is my, is my answers.

& she looks into it & sees herself, standing there, on both sides of the mirror.

She is my she, she says.

Little strangers. Little doppelgängers. Separated at birth & now together.

She stands on both sides of the mirror, twinned, filled with grief for the years she spent carrying herself around like a poison or a secret & elated for the fact of surviving her face & shape for this minute of seeing

her all-selves—without an urge to kill or to be killed.

vi. the book of one small thing

Ars Poetica

May the poems be
the little snail's trail.

Everywhere I go,
every inch: quiet record

of the foot's silver prayer.
        I lived once.
        Thank you.
        It was here.

Notes

"St. Elizabeth" takes place in the St. Elizabeth parish of Jamaica. In the Christian & Islamic traditions, Elizabeth is the mother of John the Baptist/ Yahya. Elizabeth & her husband, Zacharia, could not conceive of a child for most of their lives. As a gift from god, Elizabeth & Zacharia were given a son.

The sentence "One day it will be otherwise" from the poem "Central City Senior Center, New Orleans," is an adaptation of the last two lines of Jane Kenyon's poem "Otherwise."

In title & in spirit, "On Living" & "On Kindness" are after Nazim Hikmet.

Acknowledgments

I am tremendously grateful to the editors of the following publications, programs, & archival sites for giving these poems, some of them in earlier versions, a home before they were a collection:

A Public Space: "Praise Song for the Donkey";
BBC Radio: "Explaining the Land Mine to the Small Child";
Black Renaissance/ Renaissance Noire: "Abuelo, Mi Muerto," "Science";
Boog Reader: "Portrait of the Woman as a Skein";
Court Green: "For Patrick Rosal Who Wore a Dress & Said";
Fence: "The Dream";
From the Fishouse: "Kingdom Animalia," "Night, for Henry Dumas," "Self-Portrait as the Snake's Skin," "They Tell Me You Are Gone";
Gulf Coast: "Ode to the Little 'r,'" "Three Girls, One of Them a Coward Girl";
Huizache: "Mississippi Burial, On the Ferry to Algiers," "On Kindness";
Jangle the Threads: "I Am Not Ready to Die Yet";
So Much Things To Say: "Starlight Multiplication";
The Massachusetts Review: "This Morning the Small Bird Brought a Message from the Other Side."

I would like to express my gratitude to the Jerome Foundation. Many of these poems grew out of my travel & writing grant to Eritrea. I am also grateful to the National Endowment for the Arts, the Watson Foundation, VOA, the Joiner Center, & the Toor Cummings Center. Thank you to the Hampshire, Queens College, Drew, Volume, Calabash, LouderArts, Urban Word, & DreamYard communities, I have been taught & challenged by your work. My hand-on-my-heart gratitude to the DY Prep Slam Team (08–09), Acentos, & Cave Canem: oh, school & family. To my students, to anyone who ever shared a poem with me or invited me to read, to everyone who has ever taught me a wise thing: thank you.

My particular gratitude goes to: Chris Abani, Elizabeth Alexander, Rhianna Almendras, Elana Bell, Haile Berhe, Tara Betts, Amina Blacksher, Christian Campbell, Ama Codjoe, Johanny DeLeon, Toi Derricotte, Cornelius Eady,

Araia Ephrem, David Flores, Tanya Gallo, Daphne & Saultas Gibbs, Huriy Ghirmai, Dagoberto Gilb, Rachel Eliza Griffiths, Dariana Gomez, Ellen Hagan, Samuel Harman, Haydil Henriquez, Steffie Kinglake, Michele Kotler, Paola Marcus Carranza, Anna Molitor, Erin Molitor, John Murillo, Allison Myers, Chris Myers, Stephanos Papadopoulos, Irene Prestianary, Rassan Salandy, Erynn Sampson, Ruth Irupé Sanabria, Samantha Thornhill, Markus Underwood, Rich Villar, Simone White, Marina Wilson. Thank you to: Peter Conners, Sandy Knight, & BOA Editions, for caring for this manuscript & treating me so kindly; Kamilah Aisha Moon, for your words, always, & for twice saying, *Send it*; to Laure-Anne Bosselaar for saying, *Yes*; Patrick Rosal & Ross Gay, for your poems & eyes; Carla Repice, for the animal of this cover; Nikky Finney, Sandy Taylor, & Martín Espada, for seeing me.

My love & my thank you: Girmay Keleta, Angelita Serrano Vargas, Yosef, Banna, Ariana, Negisti, the Aunts & the Uncles, the cousins, my All.

About the Author

Aracelis Girmay was born & raised in Southern California, with roots in Puerto Rico, Eritrea, & African America. She is the author of the collage-based picture book *changing, changing* & the poetry collection *Teeth*, for which she was awarded a GLCA New Writers Award. Girmay has taught youth writing workshops in schools & community centers for the past ten years. She is assistant professor of poetry writing at Hampshire College & also teaches in the low-residency MFA program at Drew University. Girmay is a Cave Canem Fellow & an Acentos board member.

BOA Editions, Ltd.
American Poets Continuum Series

No. 1   *The Fuhrer Bunker: A Cycle of Poems in Progress*
W. D. Snodgrass

No. 2   *She*
M. L. Rosenthal

No. 3   *Living With Distance*
Ralph J. Mills, Jr.

No. 4   *Not Just Any Death*
Michael Waters

No. 5   *That Was Then: New and Selected Poems*
Isabella Gardner

No. 6   *Things That Happen Where There Aren't Any People*
William Stafford

No. 7   *The Bridge of Change: Poems 1974–1980*
John Logan

No. 8   *Signatures*
Joseph Stroud

No. 9   *People Live Here: Selected Poems 1949–1983*
Louis Simpson

No. 10   *Yin*
Carolyn Kizer

No. 11   *Duhamel: Ideas of Order in Little Canada*
Bill Tremblay

No. 12   *Seeing It Was So*
Anthony Piccione

No. 13   *Hyam Plutzik: The Collected Poems*

No. 14   *Good Woman: Poems and a Memoir 1969–1980*
Lucille Clifton

No. 15   *Next: New Poems*
Lucille Clifton

No. 16   *Roxa: Voices of the Culver Family*
William B. Patrick

No. 17   *John Logan: The Collected Poems*

No. 18   *Isabella Gardner: The Collected Poems*

No. 19   *The Sunken Lightship*
Peter Makuck

No. 20   *The City in Which I Love You*
Li-Young Lee

No. 21   *Quilting: Poems 1987–1990*
Lucille Clifton

No. 22   *John Logan: The Collected Fiction*

No. 23   *Shenandoah and Other Verse Plays*
Delmore Schwartz

No. 24   *Nobody Lives on Arthur Godfrey Boulevard*
Gerald Costanzo

No. 25   *The Book of Names: New and Selected Poems*
Barton Sutter

No. 26   *Each in His Season*
W. D. Snodgrass

No. 27   *Wordworks: Poems Selected and New*
Richard Kostelanetz

No. 28   *What We Carry*
Dorianne Laux

No. 29   *Red Suitcase*
Naomi Shihab Nye

No. 30   *Song*
Brigit Pegeen Kelly

No. 31   *The Fuehrer Bunker: The Complete Cycle*
W. D. Snodgrass

No. 32   *For the Kingdom*
Anthony Piccione

No. 33   *The Quicken Tree*
Bill Knott

No. 34   *These Upraised Hands*
William B. Patrick

No. 35 *Crazy Horse in Stillness*
William Heyen

No. 36 *Quick, Now, Always*
Mark Irwin

No. 37 *I Have Tasted the Apple*
Mary Crow

No. 38 *The Terrible Stories*
Lucille Clifton

No. 39 *The Heat of Arrivals*
Ray Gonzalez

No. 40 *Jimmy & Rita*
Kim Addonizio

No. 41 *Green Ash, Red Maple, Black Gum*
Michael Waters

No. 42 *Against Distance*
Peter Makuck

No. 43 *The Night Path*
Laurie Kutchins

No. 44 *Radiography*
Bruce Bond

No. 45 *At My Ease: Uncollected Poems of the Fifties and Sixties*
David Ignatow

No. 46 *Trillium*
Richard Foerster

No. 47 *Fuel*
Naomi Shihab Nye

No. 48 *Gratitude*
Sam Hamill

No. 49 *Diana, Charles, & the Queen*
William Heyen

No. 50 *Plus Shipping*
Bob Hicok

No. 51 *Cabato Sentora*
Ray Gonzalez

No. 52 *We Didn't Come Here for This*
William B. Patrick

No. 53 *The Vandals*
Alan Michael Parker

No. 54 *To Get Here*
Wendy Mnookin

No. 55 *Living Is What I Wanted: Last Poems*
David Ignatow

No. 56 *Dusty Angel*
Michael Blumenthal

No. 57 *The Tiger Iris*
Joan Swift

No. 58 *White City*
Mark Irwin

No. 59 *Laugh at the End of the World: Collected Comic Poems 1969–1999*
Bill Knott

No. 60 *Blessing the Boats: New and Selected Poems: 1988–2000*
Lucille Clifton

No. 61 *Tell Me*
Kim Addonizio

No. 62 *Smoke*
Dorianne Laux

No. 63 *Parthenopi: New and Selected Poems*
Michael Waters

No. 64 *Rancho Notorious*
Richard Garcia

No. 65 *Jam*
Joe-Anne McLaughlin

No. 66 *A. Poulin, Jr. Selected Poems*
Edited, with an Introduction by Michael Waters

No. 67 *Small Gods of Grief*
Laure-Anne Bosselaar

No. 68 *Book of My Nights*
Li-Young Lee

No. 69 *Tulip Farms and Leper Colonies*
Charles Harper Webb

No. 70 *Double Going*
Richard Foerster

No. 71 *What He Took*
Wendy Mnookin

No. 72 *The Hawk Temple at Tierra Grande*
Ray Gonzalez

117

Colophon

The Isabella Gardner Poetry Award is given biennially to a poet in mid-career with a new book of exceptional merit. Poet, actress, and associate editor of *Poetry* magazine, Isabella Gardner (1915–1981) published five celebrated collections of poetry, was three times nominated for the National Book Award, and was the first recipient of the New York State Walt Whitman Citation of Merit for Poetry. She championed the work of young and gifted poets, helping many of them to find publication.

The publication of this book is made possible, in part, by the special support of the following individuals:

Anonymous
Nin Andrews
Michael Blumenthal, *in honor of Steve Orlen*
Bernadette Catalana
Pete & Bev French
Anne Germanacos
Suzanne Gouvernet
Robert E. Horn, M.D.
Robin, Hollon & Casey Hursh, *in memory of Peter Hursh*
X. J. Kennedy
Katy Lederer
Deborah Ronnen & Sherman Levey
Rosemary & Lew Lloyd
Dorianne Laux & Joseph Millar, *in memory of Lucille Clifton*
Michael Waters & Mihaela Moscaliuc
Janice N. Harrington & Robert Dale Parker
Boo Poulin, *in honor of Sandi Henschel*
Steven O. Russell & Phyllis Rifkin-Russell
Vicki & Richard Schwartz
Gerald Vorrasi, *in memory of Greg Liphard*
Ellen & David Wallack
Glenn & Helen William